Stand Up for God
Biblical Principles Learned in a Military Career

By
Michael H. Imhof,
U.S. Navy SEAL Commander (ret.)

World rights reserved. This book or any portion thereof may not be copied or reproduced in any form or manner whatever, except as provided by law, without the written permission of the publisher, except by a reviewer who may quote brief passages in a review.

The author assumes full responsibility for the accuracy of all facts and quotations as cited in this book. The opinions expressed in this book are the author's personal views and interpretations, and do not necessarily reflect those of the publisher.

This book is provided with the understanding that the publisher is not engaged in giving spiritual, legal, medical, or other professional advice. If authoritative advice is needed, the reader should seek the counsel of a competent professional.

Copyright © 2017 Michael H. Imhof

Copyright © 2017 Aspect Books

ISBN-13: 978-1-4796-0847-8 (Paperback)

ISBN-13: 978-1-4796-0848-5 (ePub)

ISBN-13: 978-1-4796-0849-2 (Mobi)

Library of Congress Control Number: 2017913588

All scripture is taken from the Authorized King James Version (KJV) unless otherwise stated. Public domain.

Scripture quotations marked (NKJV) are taken from the New King James Version®. Copyright © 1982 by Thomas Nelson. Used by permission. All rights reserved.

Scripture quotations marked (NIV) are taken from the Holy Bible, New International Version®, NIV®. Copyright © 1973, 1978, 1984, 2011 by Biblica, Inc.™ Used by permission of Zondervan. All rights reserved worldwide.

*Dedicated to my loving wife, Paulette.
She has been a great helpmate and wonderful partner in ministry.
She is a blessing from God.*

*"But be ye **doer**s of the word, and not hearers only, deceiving your own selves. For if any be a hearer of the word, and not a **doer**, he is like unto a man beholding his natural face in a glass: For he beholdeth himself, and goeth his way, and straightway forgetteth what manner of man he was."*

James 1:22–25 (KJV)

*Jesus saith unto him, **I am the way, the** truth, and **the** life: no man cometh unto **the** Father, but by me.*

John 14:6 (KJV)

Contents

Foreword		9
Introduction		11
Chapter 1:	Class 79 Experience	13
Chapter 2:	Class 80 Experience	17
Chapter 3:	Biblical Principles Learned From BUD/S Training	20
Chapter 4:	If I Can Trust Parachutes, I Can Trust God	24
Chapter 5:	Hijacked in Lebanon: A Spiritual Principle Learned	27
Chapter 6:	When I Worked with Soviet Union Officers	31
Chapter 7:	Why I Stopped Drinking	34
Chapter 8:	Why I Stopped Cursing	37
Chapter 9:	Harassment Commonplace	40
Chapter 10:	Forgiveness Mandatory	42
Chapter 11:	Behavior Sometimes Peculiar as a Christian	45
Chapter 12:	Preparation and Study Common	47
Chapter 13:	Stand Up for God	49
Various Photos		53
Conclusion		62

Foreword

A principle may be defined as an accepted or professed rule of action or conduct. Living by quality principles will help create character. As I pondered much of my military career, I considered how so many things I went through, and learned from, pointed to biblical principles in the Bible. The Bible shows us God in so many ways. God and His Word are one. Thus, these principles showed me some glimpses of God's nature, and His perspective on some aspects of human life.

In essence, everything one needs to know to be successful is in God's Word. As one applies biblical principles, and does things God's way, one will move forward in a positive direction in life because God's ways are always best for us—as individuals, as a group, or as a nation. One will become wise as one becomes a doer of the Word. I say this with complete confidence because God always honors His Word.

There are many more biblical principles one can glean from the Bible; I've only provided some that I personally learned from my military and paramilitary experiences. As you read your Bible, and receive sound biblical teaching, you'll gain insight into many more.

Just looking at society tells us clearly how important principles are. Those who follow solid biblical principles will show the positive fruits of those principles in their lives. Those who don't often end up ruining their lives, land in jail, or fall far short of their potential in life.

It's pretty simple. Live your life in accordance with biblical principles, and you'll become known as an individual with strong character and moral values. Your reputation will be perceived as honorable as others will attest, and a reputation is something that you can't buy or sell. It's gained from the way you live, and it speaks volumes about you and who you are.

Michael H. Imhof
Commander, U.S. Navy (ret.)

Introduction

I put off doing this book for some time. I had thoughts about doing it, but just put it off until recently when the Holy Spirit moved on my heart to put words on paper. I resisted for a while, thinking perhaps it was just me, until I realized that the Lord was working with me to do this.

I'm confident that there are many books and written materials on the subject of principles. So why should I write one on this subject since there is already plenty of material out there? First, God has His reasons for me doing this, and second, biblical principles I gleaned were based on personal military and paramilitary experiences. This creates testimony, and others can greatly benefit from testimonies. Testimonies often encourage one's faith when they see the goodness of God demonstrated in the lives of other people. God is not a respecter of persons, and what He'll do for one, He'll do for others. God is not capricious; He's consistent to His Word and values.

There's one thing about truth. It's absolute and it always proves its course. The Bible is God's truth to us. It's really our owner's manual for life. We need to live our lives in accordance with its teaching. To shun God's Word, and live in opposition to it, is foolery.

This work is pretty simple and to the point. It's not extensive in length and it's easy to read. That said, as you read the pages, please examine the principles alluded to as you ponder them in your heart. In light of God's Word, what is He attempting to communicate to you? If adjustments need to be made, then make them. You'll be the better for it.

God loves you so much. Know this is true. He only wants the best for you, and wants to do good things in your life. As you build biblical principles into your life, this will lead to godly character.

Chapter 1
Class 79 Experience

I started Basic Underwater Demolition/SEAL (BUD/S) training at the Naval Amphibious Base in Coronado, California, with Class 79 during 1974. I graduated from BUD/S training with Class 80 in January of 1975. Class 79 was after Class 78. That's easy to understand; however, there's an intriguing aspect to that statement. Class 78 was known as the class that never was. How can that be? It's because no one graduated from that class. One can be rolled back due to injury, drop on request (DOR) by ringing a bell during training, or dropped by the administrative staff for performance. All personnel from Class 78 fell into one of these categories.

BUD/S training, at that time, was divided into three phases—Physical Fitness; Land Warfare/Demolition; and Dive phases. Training was about six months in duration. The end of the first phase culminated in what was known as Hell Week. This week consists of cold, wet, brutally difficult operational training on exceptionally little sleep during the course of the week. Per NAVYSEALS.com, "Hell Week tests physical endurance, mental toughness, pain and cold tolerance, teamwork, attitude, and your ability to perform work under high physical and mental stress, and sleep deprivation. Above all, it tests determination and desire."

> *"Hell Week tests physical endurance, mental toughness, pain and cold tolerance, teamwork, attitude, and your ability to perform work under high physical and mental stress, and sleep deprivation. Above all, it tests determination and desire."*
>
> —*NAVYSEALS.com*

As previously mentioned, I started with Class 79. So how is it that I graduated with Class 80? I was in the middle of Hell Week during First Phase (Physical Fitness). We were conducting a night swim in San Diego Bay. Although I was keeping up in the swim, I told my swim buddy that I was having a hard time breathing (we swam with swim buddies as a safety factor). My swim buddy motioned for the safety boat to come over. I explained my breathing situation to the instructors on the safety boat. Before I knew it, I was pulled onboard from the water, and taken by ambulance over Coronado Bridge to Balboa Hospital in San Diego.

I was kept there overnight and I'm confident I slept quite soundly. As I recall, I was diagnosed with asphyxia pneumonia. In other words, water had gotten into my lungs, and apparently, was robbing my lungs of oxygen. As I was kept there for observation and recovery during the next day, I remember arguing with the doctors and nurses, pleading my case to let me out of the hospital so I could get back with my training class. I remember a friend from a different class came to the hospital and encouraged me to try and get back with Class 79 so I wouldn't have to do Hell Week again.

Eventually, after a period of time, I'm not sure how, I was allowed to leave. I eventually made it back over Coronado Bridge to the Naval Amphibious Base. I remember finally locating my class on the Naval Amphibious Base grounds. I approached the instructors telling them that I didn't quit and that I wanted to get back with the class. Unfortunately, I was told by the instructors present that I had missed some of Hell Week and that I would be rolled back to Class 80. My morale sunk very low. It was a depressive moment. In other words, I would have to start training over and go through Hell Week again.

I do recall an interesting event during this particular Hell Week before I was taken to Balboa Hospital. We were doing night surf passage through the surf zone with our inflatable boat small (IBS). We had seven men in the boat. All needed to paddle for us to make it through the surf zone. I remember one individual in the front of the boat became mesmerized by this huge plunging wave coming towards us. He held his paddle to the side and did not paddle as he became focused on this huge wave. As could be expected, the wave lifted us up and washed us ashore, with bodies thrown out of the boat and paddles flying. This event stressed the importance of teamwork. All working together was exceptionally important.

So often we get into trouble when we look at the circumstances. My classmate became mesmerized by the huge wave coming towards us. This story reminded me

> *The Bible is our reference for living. I sometimes think of it as our owner's manual for life.*

of Peter when he was walking on the water towards Jesus. Peter began to look at the waves, and fear set in. He began to sink. Isn't that like all of us in life? We look and become mesmerized by the circumstances instead of staying focused on God's Word. We must base our faith on the Word of God continually and not be swayed by circumstances or appearances. What does the Word of God say? We must always side with God's Word. The Bible is our reference for living. I sometimes think of it as our owner's manual for life. We must live our lives in accordance with the Word of God. Matthew 7:24-27 says, "Therefore whosoever heareth these sayings of mine, and **doeth them**, I will liken him unto a wise man, which **built his house upon a rock**: And the rain descended, and the floods came, and the winds blew, and beat upon that house; and it fell not: for it was **founded upon a rock**. And every one that heareth these sayings of mine, and doeth them not, shall be likened unto a foolish man, which built his house upon the sand."

When a situation comes up in one's life, one needs to refer to the Bible. One needs to ask oneself, *what does the Bible say about my situation?* It's our bedrock for living. Mark 13:31 says, "Heaven and earth shall pass away: but **my words shall not pass away.**" This means that God will always honor His Word.

Chapter 2
Class 80 Experience

I was told by the instructors that I would be Class Leader for a while for Class 80 so a more senior officer could have more time to work on his physical fitness. It turned out that I would do this until Hell Week. At that time, he would take Class Leader position and I would become a Boat Crew Commander for Hell Week. Although I liked the thought of this, I also was apprehensive about it because I knew the instructors would really harass me even more because of the position. So thus, I assumed Class Leadership up to Hell Week for Class 80.

I remember during First Phase training one officer had a watch on during morning physical fitness training. It was dark and I had not checked him for wearing a watch. One of the instructors noticed it, and told me to go get wet in the ocean because he was not supposed to have a watch on. In other words, I was responsible for my men. I proceeded to run to the ocean, jump in, and come back to the training area to resume the exercises.

On another occasion, we were doing a soft sand run on the Silver Strand beach. Running in the soft sand takes a fair amount of effort and one is apt to gasp for air if there is a quick pace. The instructors were pushing the class and there was a lull in Jodi calls. Jodi calls are group chants to express esprit de corps and teamwork. Often times I would lead these Jodi calls, but as I said, there was a lull during a stretch of this particular soft sand run. All of a sudden, I was told to go jump in the ocean and get wet. I did so, and then I ran to catch up with the class. I was being held responsible for the class since I was the acting Class Leader at the time. There were not enough Jodi calls.

Hell Week for Class 80 started on a Sunday evening, and finally culminated on the following Saturday afternoon. I remember getting just a little sleep on Friday evening of that week. Hell Week keeps one constantly moving and doing things. Running, rubber boat training, obstacle course, land operations, swimming, log physical training, and other areas of training are conducted during this week. One is always on the go, and of course, harassment from the instructors commonly takes place. It's a grind that one must endure as instructors are checking for desire and determination.

Are you going to quit? The instructors want you to quit now if you're going to quit as opposed to getting assigned to a SEAL Team and then quitting on an operation. There's rhyme and reason to why they push you during a week of training of this nature. It's typical for people to drop out during Hell Week for each BUD/S training class. It's designed to weed people out.

> *Are you going to quit? The instructors want you to quit now if you're going to quit as opposed to getting assigned to a SEAL Team and then quitting on an operation.*

I can remember finishing Hell Week on that Saturday afternoon. When I got back to my quarters, I went to bed after a quick shower and woke up late Sunday afternoon to go to the rest room. It was a deep and solid sleep. My body was exceptionally tired. I then proceeded to have a great sleep for the rest of Sunday evening.

As I recall this Hell Week, I still remember the instructors yelling at us through bull horns from the shoreline as we were doing IBS passage over the Hotel Del Coronado rocks on Coronado

Beach. We were outside the surf zone and were being called into land. Our objective was to pass over the rocks. I told my boat crew that we were going to take our time, pick the right rhythm between waves, and proceed. Many students have suffered injuries on these rocks when doing this evolution during training. We worked together, got over the rocks as a team, and met the instructors ashore. The key to this success was working together as a unit. This was symbolic of the teamwork required for the many evolutions that we went through during Hell Week.

Chapter 3
Biblical Principles Learned From BUD/S Training

Four key principles immediately come to mind when I think of biblical principles I learned from BUD/S training. They are perseverance, to be strong, responsibility, and teamwork, or unity of effort.

First, there's the principle of perseverance. Romans 5:4 states, "and **perseverance**, character; and character, hope" (NKJV). 2 Timothy 3:10 says, "But you have carefully followed my doctrine, manner of life, purpose, faith, longsuffering, love, **perseverance**" (NKJV). 2 Peter 1:6 states, "to knowledge self-control, to self-control **perseverance**, to **perseverance** godliness" (NKJV).

Perseverance is important to succeed in one's endeavors and life. In a Christian's walk, it is essential. It's a godly principle. The world and its system is constantly pushing against one's walk as a Christian. Daily, one must resist the temptations of pleasures or compromise. I remember when I've swum in the ocean. I often had to swim against a current. If I did not swim, that current would push me back. I had to swim to make progress.

One must persevere as a Christian because just the cares of this life and developing or emergent situations will challenge any-

Chapter 3 Biblical Principles Learned From BUD/S Training

one. One must persist with positive attitude, and never surrender. God will be there to help us. We must trust in Him and never give up, but persist in our daily Christian walk against any situation of adversity or challenge.

Second, I learned from BUD/S training to be strong. Of course, the Bible makes it quite clear that as a Christian I'm to be strong. Romans 15:1 states, "We then who are **strong** ought to bear with the scruples of the weak, and not to please ourselves" (NKJV). 1 Corinthians 16:13 says, "Watch, stand fast in the faith, be brave, be **strong**" (NKJV). 2 Timothy 2:1 states, "You therefore, my son, be **strong** in the grace that is in Christ Jesus" (NKJV).

A Christian's walk is not for the timid. We are to be strong as directed by the Word of God. A husband needs to be strong for his wife and family, and a wife needs to be strong for her husband and family. One encounters many storms in life: spiritual, financial, health-related, marital, job-related, neighbor disputes, concerns over the future, and others. Even so, we are to be strong and not have our faith shaken. We are to remain steadfast and faithful to the Lord regardless of any circumstance. Nothing this world offers is worth the priceless gift God has given us through our salvation. 2 Corinthians 2:14 makes it clear: "Now thanks be unto God, which **always causeth us to triumph in Christ,** and maketh manifest the savour of his knowledge by us in every place." We always triumph in Christ Jesus as we remain strong in Him and trust in His Word.

Third, I learned responsibility. It's pretty clear what scripture has to say about this. 1 Corinthians 7:24 tells us, "Brothers and sisters,

One will never mature in life until one takes responsibility for one's actions and decisions.

each person, as **responsible** to God, should remain in the situation they were in when God called them" (NIV). Acts 6:3 says, "Brothers and sisters, choose seven men from among you who are known to be full of the Spirit and wisdom. We will turn this **responsibility** over to them" (NIV).

The story of Adam and Eve gives a great example of responsibility. God came down to the Garden of Eden and called out for Adam. Of course, at this time, Adam and Eve had already eaten of the forbidden fruit and had sinned. Notice that God called for Adam and not Eve. Adam responded by blaming the sin on the woman and didn't take responsibility for his decision. *It's not my fault, God, it's her fault.* How common this is in the world today! It's not my fault, it's someone else's fault. One will never mature in life until one takes responsibility for one's actions and decisions. There's something to remember about mediocre people: they want authority, but not accountability.

Back to the point that God called for Adam, not Eve. Men are to be responsible leaders in their home. I often say that a two-headed snake is a freak. In other words, someone has to be the headship. Husbands and wives are to submit to each other, but someone ultimately has to be responsible for direction. Men are to love their wives and wives are to respect their husbands. No one lords over the other. There needs to be the mutual love of God at work in a marriage where the needs of each are taken into account.

Let me say this another way. If a U.S. Navy ship runs aground on a coral reef, typically, there will be an investigation. Even if a Lieutenant was on the bridge when the mishap occurred and the Captain of the ship was not, it's common for the Captain of the ship to be held responsible. He is the leader on the ship; thus, he bears the ultimate responsibility for decisions made. Everyone can't be in charge, so he bears that burden.

I recall a story from nature that I read in a book one time. Someone was observing these crows. It seems a flock of crows flew down into a field with some food remains from the crops. Two crows posted themselves as sentries on tree branches. Then, all of a sudden, a predator started to approach without the sentries detecting the threat. One of the crows in the field somehow noticed the threat and the flock suddenly lifted as a result and escaped the danger. It was interesting to note that birds from the flock then flew toward the sentries and attacked them. The lesson was clear. The flock was holding the sentries responsible for not doing their duty. They were to observe for threats, and the threat went unnoticed.

Fourth, I learned how important teamwork, or unity of effort, is. Biblically speaking, unity among the brethren is exceptionally stressed in the Bible. Ephesians 4:3 states, "endeavoring to keep the **unity** of the Spirit in the bond of peace." Ephesians 4:13 says, "till we all come to the **unity** of the faith and of the knowledge of the Son of God, to a perfect man, to the measure of the stature of the fullness of Christ," and Ephesians 4:16 continues with, "from whom the whole body, joined and knit together by what every joint supplies, according to the **effective working by which every part does its share**, causes growth of the body for the edifying of itself in love" (NKJV).

I grew up outside Buffalo, New York. Buffalo is known for having lake effect snow off Lake Erie during the winter months. I can recall many winter storms and much snowfall. That said, one easily notices that a snowflake by itself is extremely fragile, but put a lot of snowflakes together, and they stop traffic. That's unity. There is strength in unity and weakness in disunity.

The Book of Nehemiah gives us a great biblical example of unity of effort. Having heard that the walls of Jerusalem had not been rebuilt, and having received permission from King Artaxerxes to go to Jerusalem to rebuild the walls, Nehemiah demonstrated great leadership and managerial skills in the accomplishment of this task. The rebuilding of the walls was accomplished in fifty-two days in the face of angry opposition from Sanballat the Horonite, Tobiah the Ammonite, and others. It was an amazing feat that was accomplished through the efforts of people in one accord.

A leader who gets his objectives into the hearts of his people, and gets them working together, will greatly benefit from those efforts. It points towards success.

Chapter 4
If I Can Trust Parachutes, I Can Trust God

Trust is a firm belief in the reliability, truth, ability, or strength of someone or something. There's an assurance, confidence, or faith in trust. With that in mind, I want to address the subject of trust.

I made over one hundred parachute jumps in my military career. I initially attended the U.S. Army Basic Airborne School in Ft. Benning, Georgia, where I first received training in static line parachute operations. Later, I received free-fall training while assigned at SEAL Team TWO.

In either case, one has to trust that parachute to open when one jumps out of the airplane. There is trust in that parachute. If that parachute does not open, then one will probably fall to their death as a result.

Consider a free fall operation. In free fall, one jumps out of the aircraft with no connection to the aircraft whatsoever. In static line, one attaches the parachute static line to a cable. When one falls, that static line pulls out the parachute for the jumper as the jumper falls. Again, with free fall there is no connection whatsoever. Thousands of feet up in the air one is totally trusting that parachute to open when one leaves the aircraft. That's an awesome thought.

As my memory goes back to these parachute operations, I consider how sometimes we don't fully trust God as we should. Mark 13:31 says, "Heaven and earth shall pass away: but **my words shall not pass away**." In other words, God will always honor his Word. Proverbs 3:5–6 states, "**Trust in the LORD with all thine heart**; and lean not unto thine own understanding. In all thy ways acknowledge him, and he shall direct thy paths." **We are to fully trust God.**

If I can trust a parachute to open while thousands of feet above the earth in open air, then I should be able to fully trust God. Here's what happens though. We allow our minds to dwell on negative thoughts, and to sometimes fall into fear and doubt. Fear is opposite of faith and will rob us of blessings if we allow it to. Demonic opposition will use fear and doubt against us and we must guard against it, and send it away. 2 Timothy 1:7 says, "**For God hath not given us the spirit of fear**; but of power, and of love, and of a sound mind." A spirit of fear never comes from God. God is a God of faith.

Your eyes and ears are keys to your heart (or spirit). What you see and hear goes into your heart. We must therefore plant good seed—the Word of God—into our hearts. Romans 10:17 tells us, "So then **faith cometh by hearing**, and **hearing by** the word of God." This means you get faith by hearing. Conversely, listening to negative words contrary to God's Word will lead to doubt and fear, and rob you of what you're believing God to do.

Joshua understood from God how life could be successful. In Joshua 1:8 God instructed Joshua as follows, "This book of the law shall not depart out of thy mouth; but thou shalt **meditate therein day and night, that thou mayest observe to do according to all that is written therein: for then thou shalt make thy way prosperous, and then thou shalt have good success**." As we honor and trust God's Word, we see victory. Why? Because God always honors His Word.

Sometimes people wonder if the Bible is really true and can be trusted. One of the things I came to realize was that the Bible is the only holy book in the world that I know of that uses prophecy. The others, like the Quran and Hindu holy books, don't, but the Bible does. That alone sets it apart. Not that God needs an apologetic, but the Bible is backed up by history and archeological evidence time and time again. This is not a pie in the sky book. The Bible is God-breathed, and prophecy proves it. Basically, man records history but God writes it.

I've lived in Israel, Jordan, Egypt, Sinai, and worked in Southern Lebanon for different periods of time. Geographically the Bible became alive to me. During these times, I became acquainted with many different biblical sites. As I researched these areas, saw what God's Word said about them, and then comprehended how history and archeological evidence again and again proved God's Word, I was amazed. If you don't believe me, then I encourage you to go to these many different areas, and hear what the tour guides have to say about them. Either that, or research this subject, and you'll see that history and archeological evidence back up the Bible.

When I hear some question about the validity of the Bible, or even the reality of God, I consider some basic pragmatic reasoning. How can there be a God? Anything man has created has been done by an intelligent mind, or reasoning. Sometimes there will be a series of systems which provide desired results. Whether it be an automobile, kitchen stove, washing machine, television set, or something else, an intelligent mind was behind the design.

That said, man's blood system is more complex than anything man has ever created. We're surrounded by a series of systems that keep things working together in efficiency. Gravity, centrifugal force, biological, zoological, and other systems work together with each other in giving balance and sustainability on earth. This kind of order does not come out of chaos.

In summation, there is a God who honors His Word, and loves us with a great love. We need to free fall into His arms and trust His Word to sustain us.

Chapter 5
Hijacked in Lebanon: A Spiritual Principle Learned

On December 17, 1981, I was hijacked at gunpoint in Southern Lebanon. After reviewing what happened to me years later I realized a spiritual principle was in effect without me knowing it. It's true that God protected me; but, I believe that protection was initially generated by my proclaimed words before I ever arrived on Middle Eastern soil.

I was a young Christian, and I was getting ready to be assigned to the United Nations Truce Supervision Organization (UNTSO) in the Middle East for a one-year tour of duty as a United Nations (UN) observer.

As a young Navy Lieutenant, I was looking forward to this assignment. It was my first overseas assignment and I was going to Israel, Egypt, Jordan, and Lebanon for duty. I also would be working with different nationalities. I was excited about this assignment to say the least.

My parents and others were concerned about my safety and I told them that I was going to be all right. I told them and others that I believed that I was going to come back safely. Within me, I believed this to be so and my words proclaimed what I believed.

I repeated words of this nature numerous times before I left the United States for Israel during July 1981. Dick Mills, a man of God, had given me some scriptures prior to this assignment regarding safety and I had locked them into my heart.

I initially arrived at Tel Aviv, and then proceeded to Jerusalem for in-processing. My first assignment was for about two and one-half months in Cairo, Egypt. I then transferred to Amman, Jordan, for two months. After Amman, Jordan, I was transferred to Nahariya, Israel, where I would work in Southern Lebanon.

As a UN observer for Observer Group Lebanon (OGL), I lived in Nahariya and went across the Southern Lebanese border for duty. I performed observation duties at different locations in Southern Lebanon as well as conducted mobile patrols. It was a rewarding experience in many ways.

On December 17, 1981, I was at an observation post in Southern Lebanon with another American officer and a Swedish officer. The Swedish officer and I proceeded to go on a mobile patrol. The American officer remained behind at the observation post. The Swedish officer had been assigned to OGL for a much longer period than I. He served as the driver, and I communicated via radio at different checkpoints to home base. Communication at the checkpoints was a safety measure to protect and track the observers in this potentially dangerous area of operations.

Different sects live in Lebanon. There were the Druze, Sunni Muslims, Shiite Muslims, Maronite Christians, and others as well. Sometimes it was tough to determine what group people belonged to unless someone told you or you asked them. Some people were friendly to Americans while others were not so friendly.

The Swedish Officer and I departed in the jeep from our observation post. En route, I communicated at fixed points back to home base via radio, as was standard procedure. Up ahead, to the side of the road, was a white vehicle with its hood up. There were three Middle Eastern men looking under the hood. As we slowed to pass them, all of a sudden they jumped out with weapons pointed at us. I could barely grab the radio hand-set when I had an AK-47 pointing towards my head. I released the radio as the Swedish Officer and I were directed to get out of the vehicle.

Chapter 5 Hijacked in Lebanon: A Spiritual Principle Learned

As UN observers we did not carry weapons. We were marched down the side of a hill about 10–15 yards apart for perhaps 70 yards with our hands up and weapons pointed at our backs. The three Middle Eastern men decided not to shoot us, then abruptly left us, took our vehicle, and departed. It's interesting: I even had a U.S. flag on the sleeve of my uniform in full view so it was apparent that I was an American. I mention this since some groups or people in that region didn't like Americans. Although I could have easily been taken hostage, I was not. (One may recall that Lieutenant Colonel Rich Higgins, who served with the same UN organization, was taken captive during February 1988 in the same area of operations and later executed.)

The spiritual law I learned from this incident was that our words have a direct effect on our destiny. The truth of Mark 11:23 became a reality to me as I analyzed what transpired that day under God's protection. I believed in my heart and set things in motion with my words before I ever arrived on Southern Lebanese soil.

Mark 11:23 says, "For assuredly, I say to you, whoever **says** to this mountain, 'Be removed and be cast into the sea,' and does not doubt in his heart, but **believes** that those things he **says** will be done, he will have whatever he **says**" (NKJV). Notice "**believe**" is mentioned once, but "**says**" is mentioned three times.

> *I believed in my heart and set things in motion with my words before I ever arrived on Southern Lebanese soil.*

Proverbs 18:21 states, "**Death and life** are in the power of the tongue, and those who love it will eat its fruit" (NKJV).

I would later apply this principle when I went to other high threat areas in the world like Afghanistan and Somalia. I've seen God's protection in my life on multiple occasions, and I thank Him for His faithfulness. I'm convinced that our words are instrumental in our lives, and will affect our destiny.

Believe in your heart, and confess with your mouth, are words to live by. Most assuredly, I believe that it's important to **get the promises of God firm in our hearts**, and then **speak words to affirm those promises and what we're standing for**.

One may wonder how they can better get a promise of God into their heart. Meditation on the Word of God will greatly assist as one ponders, repeats, and dwells on what the Bible is saying. Consider and concentrate on what the Word of God is saying to you. Once one gets it into their heart, then one should continue to affirm and proclaim it with their words. There's power in this connection.

Chapter 6

When I Worked with Soviet Union Officers

In the early part of that assignment with UNTSO I was assigned to Observer Group Egypt (OGE) from July to September of 1981. I was working with different nationalities which also included officers from the Soviet Union. These were Leonid Brezhnev years, so the Cold War was still in solid operation. By the way, the language for the UN operations was English, so it was easier for Americans to communicate with these different nationalities, as all were required to speak English.

I lived in Heliopolis, Egypt, a suburb of Cairo, during this assignment. Besides being assigned with officers from other countries, I would be going on observation post duty in Ismailia, Egypt, with Soviet Union officers as well. I enjoyed this experience as a young U.S. Naval officer from the United States.

Military personnel from the United States and Soviet Union were not allowed to go into the Sinai for assignments at OGE. Personnel from both nations were limited to certain duties in Ismailia, by the Suez Canal.

I remember on one assignment being assigned with three Russian officers. It was a remarkable opportunity to have direct interface. While on observation duty, each team member took time to cook for all members present during their specific, designated night. Interesting things were discussed, with points and counter points to each discussion. They called me "Misha," Russian for "Bear." It's basically their translation for Michael or Mike. Even when I think back to this time period, I still recall some of the Russian names vividly in my mind.

The Russians had different personalities like the Americans had different personalities. Some were serious, and some were quite humorous. **I learned that people are people with the same needs.**

No matter where you go in the world, this basic principle pertains to all. There may be some differences in culture and approach to life, but man's basic needs remain the same throughout the world, no matter where you're from, what language you speak, or how you were educated.

Of this I know—all need Jesus. That's why the Word says to go into all the world and make disciples. Mark 16:15–16 states, "And he said unto them, Go ye into all the world, and **preach the gospel to every creature**. He that believeth and is baptized shall be saved; but he that believeth not shall be damned."

Acts 4:12 says, "Neither is there salvation in any other: for there is **none other name under heaven given among men, whereby we must be saved**." This is referring to Jesus. Jesus is not a way; He's the only way to salvation based on the Word.

Sometimes people will question, "How can you say that Jesus is the only way to salvation?" What about someone born into an Islamic culture in Southern Egypt, or in a Brazilian rain forest among the Indian tribes? First, we are not the judge; that's God's business, not ours. We're just the messengers. We don't save anyone—that's God's job. Second, this we know, that God is a righteous God, and He will judge righteously. That's His business. He sees all hearts; however, I do believe God does expect more of those who know more.

Psalm 19:1 states, "The **heavens declare** the glory of God; and the **firmament shows His handiwork**" (NKJV). Psalm 50:6 says,

Chapter 6 When I Worked with Soviet Union Officers

"Let the **heavens declare** His righteousness, for **God Himself is Judge**" (NKJV). Psalm 97:6 further tells us, "The **heavens declare** His righteousness, and **all the peoples see His glory**" (NKJV).

Sometimes people deflect attention away from themselves by referring to someone born into another culture or religion. This is a tactful way to get the attention off of themselves. In other words, what are they now going to do with the gospel? What are they going to do about acceptance of salvation through Jesus Christ? This should be their main focus; yet, they'll focus on someone else, and not themselves, in order to give themselves an out from having to face this quality and life changing decision.

I came to the above conclusions as a result of conversations I had with a female U.S. Navy Lieutenant Commander when I was assigned to Naval Special Warfare Command. She communicated in a highly intelligent manner, but in reality, was trying to deflect attention away from herself and what she was going to do with the gospel of Jesus Christ.

This question pertains to all mankind—what are you going to do with the gospel of Jesus Christ? Someone, not saved, may say that I've heard that for 40 years now. In that case, they need to hear it one more time if they haven't accepted Jesus Christ as their Lord and Savior. For those who are saved, then the gospel story never grows old for it changes one's eternal destiny from damnation and torment in hell to everlasting life and joy in heaven. This priceless gift is free because Jesus paid the price for our sins at the cross.

Chapter 7
Why I Stopped Drinking

I was assigned to SEAL Team TWO in early 1975 in Virginia Beach, Virginia, after I graduated from BUD/S. In early 1977, I was next assigned to Underwater Demolition Team (UDT) TWENTY-ONE on the same base. In 1983, the UDT Teams were later re-designated as SEAL Teams with the UDT mission incorporated into one of the SEAL Team missions. Regardless, operational personnel assigned to either of these units would have gone through the same BUD/S basic training. The primary missions were just different.

I was a social drinker, meaning when I went out on a weekend, to a party or get together, I indulged. I was not an alcoholic. Even so, it was during this time on assignment in the Virginia Beach area that I came to receive Jesus Christ as my Lord and Savior. I made an altar call at Open Door Chapel in Virginia Beach, Virginia. Pastor Fritz Stegemann, who is now with the Lord, was the pastor at the time. He was a big man with a German background. I maintained contact with Pastor Fritz for many years that followed.

Earlier, when I was still at Frontier Central High School, God used a Fellowship of Christian Athletes (FCA) camp in Poughkeepsie, New York, to touch my heart.

Chapter 7 Why I Stopped Drinking 35

That experience always stayed deep within me. I was involved in varsity sports during high school. My wrestling coach, Charles Mead, got me to go to an FCA camp during the summer of 1968. The Lions Club sponsored me and I'm thankful for that support. I remember the camp counselors gave us a Bible at the beginning of the week and allotted some private devotional time in the mornings. I was wondering what I was going to do now. I wasn't used to reading the Bible, and I pondered what kind of a deal I got myself into. Never-the-less, as time progressed, I realized that there was something special about this week. That special presence stayed in my heart as I finished high school, went through college, and during the early years of my military career. After I made the altar call at Open Door Chapel, I finally figured out what that special presence was. It was the presence of the Holy Spirit.

Now I'll discuss the Christmas Party I went to at UDT TWENTY-ONE. I was a very young Christian and I asked a nice Christian girl to go with me as my date. I took a bottle of cold duck (an alcoholic beverage) with me to the event. I remember how I was verbally harassed for doing this. One needs to understand that I now was trying to walk the Christian life. In other words, I changed some from previous ways. Many teammates knew that I was now standing as a professed Christian. Thinking back to this time period, I can recall how, when I left the command and went home at night, that I could hardly wait to read my Bible. I had an intense desire to know more of God's Word.

"Mr. Imhof, you call yourself a Christian, and look at what you're drinking," were comments similar to what I heard that night, and many more. I felt embarrassed for myself and my date. To put it more bluntly, I believe it was the Holy Spirit dealing with me, even though evil spirits were working through them to destroy my peace.

Shortly after that experience I decided that I would not drink alcohol again. It would now be orange juice on the rocks if I went to an officer social or similar event. I realized that people were watching me closely, and I did not want anything to be a stumbling block in my witness for the Lord. Luke 6:7 states, "So the scribes and Pharisees **watched** Him closely, whether He would heal on the

Sabbath, that they might find an accusation against Him" (NKJV). Acts 9:24 says, "But their plot became known to Saul. And they **watched** the gates day and night, to kill him" (NKJV).

People are watching us as Christians. We need to be genuine, and walk the walk, and talk the talk. We need to be the best ambassadors for the Lord Jesus Christ we can possibly be. Our witness will affect others in a positive manner, or adversely. Let's affect others in positive ways. It may affect their eternal destinies, one way or the other.

Chapter 8
Why I Stopped Cursing

In my childhood I tried to maintain clean language. I was not one to curse even if I heard others do it. My mother would be quick to correct me if she heard me let a word or two slip out that was not appropriate.

I imagine my attitude on some of this was because I also went to church. I did receive some religious instruction in my youth. I grew up with a Catholic background. Often I remember my parents pushing my brother, Stevie, and I to go to church even if they didn't go. Stevie was one year younger than me. We were born on the same day, exactly one year apart. Donnie, my other brother, was eight years younger than me. I didn't have any sisters, although, my mother did have a stillborn little girl, Robin, who is now in heaven. In due time, our family will see her again.

Stevie and I would often ride our bicycles to church and back on Sunday mornings. The distance round trip was maybe three to four miles. The point is that we were receiving some religious instruction, along with parental influence in the home, to ensure we maintained clean talk.

Now, with that being said, I noticed a shift in my language once assigned to SEAL Team TWO. I was an Assistant Platoon Commander, and along with the corpsman, we were probably the youngest two personnel in the platoon. Several members of our platoon were seasoned Vietnam veterans. Talk was often coarse and laced with profanity. This, however, is not uncommon in the military. Profanity is common in the military, as it is in many areas of society.

I started to curse more and more. I thought this would enable me to influence and blend in with the platoon members in a better way. Then, in time, after I had received Jesus as my Lord and Savior, I realized that this was not right. I didn't have to compromise my values in this manner. I reasoned that I still could get my points across and accomplish my objectives without having to use profanity. I believe that the Holy Spirit was moving on my spirit.

1 Thessalonians 5:23 says, "And the very God of peace sanctify you wholly; and I pray God your whole **spirit and soul and body** be preserved blameless unto the coming of our Lord Jesus Christ". We are actually three-part beings. God primarily communicates to us through our spirits. Not only was our spirit made for God, but our spirit also has the ability to contact, receive from, and worship God. Our mind, emotion, and will make up our soul, which greatly influences our personality. Then, of course, we live in a body.

There's a phrase, "Let your conscience be your guide." Your conscience is really your spirit speaking to you. I could feel in my spirit (or conscience) that my profanity was not right, nor pleasing to God. As such, I made a conscious decision to quit cursing, and I stopped.

God's Word bears truth, and those that heed it will be the better for it.

My language from that point forward would be clean, and would edify, as opposed to displeasing the Lord. It was more important for me to please God than man. James 3:10 states, "Out of the same mouth proceed blessing and **cursing**. My brethren, **these things ought not to be so**" (NKJV). 1 Corinthians 15:33 goes on to say, "Do not be deceived: '**Evil company corrupts good habits**'" (NKJV).

Students in junior high, high school, or college, who run with the wrong crowd, often support the validity of this last scripture. Many ruin their lives by associating with the wrong people, and it need not be so. This lesson pertains to adults as well. God's Word bears truth, and those that heed it will be the better for it. In light of what I just shared, some need to give up, or sever, negative relationships. Your close friends should be ones who will encourage your faith.

Chapter 9
Harassment Commonplace

After I became a Christian in Virginia Beach, Virginia, I was considered a "Bible thumper" by many in the Teams. That was typical phraseology for that time. I would receive comments, here and there, over time because of my Christian faith.

I did my job and tried not to wear my faith on my sleeve so to speak, but people knew that I was solid in my Christian beliefs. I tried to remain firm in my walk, and be the ambassador that God would have me to be.

I remember one incident while serving as the Operations Officer of SEAL Team FIVE. A salty Master Chief Petty Officer made a comment about me going to church the coming Sunday. I thought he was trying to get to me a little bit, so I replied something like, "That's right, Master Chief, and I'll come by your house to pick you up. What time will you be ready to go?" I was letting him know that I'm confident in who I was in Christ, and that I wasn't ashamed of Jesus.

Just before I transferred from one command to another, a Petty Officer First Class told me that I had been harassed by the best and that I didn't have to take anything from anyone else. Often the words were not malicious, but were spoken in jest just to mess with me.

The verbal harassment over time actually made me a stronger Christian. We are not to be fearful of men's faces. I'm confident I became a stronger Christian as a result of those experiences. Psalm 16:8 states, "I have set the LORD ALWAYS BEFORE ME; because He is at my right hand I shall not be moved" (NKJV). 1 Corinthians 15:58 further says, "Therefore, my beloved brethren, be **steadfast**, immovable, always abounding in the work of the Lord, knowing that your labor is not in vain in the Lord" (NKJV). Hebrews 3:14 tells us, "For we have become partakers of Christ if we hold the beginning of our confidence **steadfast** to the end" (NKJV),

Chapter 10
Forgiveness Mandatory

I remember a time while serving as the Operations Officer at one of the Teams that I could easily have developed a grudge against my Commanding Officer. I worked hard and put in numerous hours in trying to satisfy him; however, sometimes I just couldn't gain his approval. Many sharp words were spoken towards me. Sometimes I would go home at night and get on my knees, asking for the Lord to help me. At times, I was just plain miserable working for this man, and desired a change from my situation.

I had to watch myself to ensure that I did not develop any grudges or harbor unforgiveness. Unforgiveness is like drinking poison and believing it's going to affect the other person. However, it's actually affecting you. Forgiveness sets us on the path towards inner healing and peace. Forgiveness is not an option; it's a directive from God. We must forgive and not allow any bitterness to take root within us.

I remember a story about a female Christian who attended a church on a regular basis. She was apparently quite active in her church. She also had good rapport with her pastor. That said, she passed away and the pastor preached at her funeral. One day, as time progressed, the pastor was spending time with the Lord around the altar. As he communed with the Lord, he made a comment to the Lord that he would like to see this sister worshipping around the throne of God. The Lord spoke back to him that she wasn't going to be there. The Lord continued to convey to the pastor that earlier in her life she had gone through a divorce and never would forgive her ex-husband from her heart. She remained bitter with unforgiveness towards him to the end.

If she wasn't going to be in heaven, then where would she be? When one leaves this world, one will either go to heaven, or to hell. The Bible repeatedly talks about both of these locations. Luke 12:5 says, "But I will forewarn you whom ye shall fear: Fear him, which after he hath killed hath power to cast into **hell**; yea, I say unto you, Fear him." Matthew 7:21 states, "Not every one that saith unto me, Lord, Lord, shall enter into the kingdom of **heaven**; but he that doeth the will of my Father which is in **heaven**."

Matthew 6:15 says, "But if ye **forgive** not men their trespasses, **neither will your Father forgive your trespasses**." Mark 11:25–26 further states, "And when ye stand praying, **forgive**, if ye have ought against any: that your Father also which is in heaven may **forgive** you your trespasses. **But if ye do not forgive, neither will your Father which is in heaven forgive your trespasses.**"

> *Unforgiveness is like drinking poison and believing it's going to affect the other person.*

I remember when the new Commanding Officer came in to replace the Commanding Officer that I mentioned earlier through a change in command. The difference was like night and day. I served as Operations Officer for both of them, and performed the same duties. With the new Commanding Officer, I had outstanding rapport and my morale immediately skyrocketed. I had a great relationship with the new Commanding Officer.

Sometimes we work with different personalities, or are placed in challenging or difficult situations where there is not much light. In those times, regardless, we must still shine our light. If we don't shine our light in those situations, then there might be complete darkness. We must be steadfast, and guard our hearts so that no bitterness or unforgiveness will take root.

This applies to life. Unforgiveness will try to pry its way into families, or into any relationship, for that matter. Unforgiveness will affect one's health and rob one's peace. If we want to maintain our peace, we must forgive. It's not only a directive from God, but ultimately, the prudent thing to do.

Luke 23:34 says, "Then said Jesus, **Father, forgive them**; for they know not what they do. And they parted his raiment, and cast lots." Jesus endured a brutal beating, and suffered an agonizing death on the cross for our sins. Even in His last moments, He prayed for His oppressors. This principle applies to us also. Forgive, and then pray for the one against you.

Anytime we're offended, it's really our pride that is hurt. It's important to walk in the confidence of who we are in God, but with a positive attitude and humility towards others. Proverbs 16:18 says, "**Pride** goeth before destruction, and an haughty spirit before a fall." James 4:6 states, "But he giveth more grace. Wherefore he saith, **God resisteth the proud**, but giveth grace unto the humble."

Be quick to repent from offense, and maintain a positive attitude. 1 John 1:9 makes it clear, "If we confess our sins, he is faithful and just to forgive us our sins, and to cleanse us from all unrighteousness." **These are words to live by—be quick to repent from offense, and choose to forgive.**

Chapter 11
Behavior Sometimes Peculiar as a Christian

Titus 2:14 states, "Who gave himself for us, that he might redeem us from all iniquity, and **purify unto himself a peculiar people, zealous of good works.**"

After my active duty military service I went overseas as a civilian in support of Department of State (DOS) or Department of Defense (DOD) operations. On one particular assignment I was serving in Liberia as Director of Training at a camp about one hour's drive outside Monrovia. We were training new recruits for the re-established Liberian Army. I was also supervisor of the camp. I had a number of personnel working for me, including some former U.S. Military members.

Some of the former U.S. Military members claimed to be Christians. Some would get on their cell phones and call their wives back in the States. Some might use SKYPE. Either way, some of these men would communicate with their wives, and then go meet girlfriends at the gate during their off times. To me, this was disheartening. First, it was sin against God. Second, it also violated their trust with their wives. It wasn't right. As Christians, we're to be faithful to God, no matter where we go and what we do. We're not to live like the world, or as the world would expect us to live.

I later would be assigned to Sudan in support of a DOS operation where I was involved in the training of some Sudanese military members. I worked with some former American military members in this assignment as well. Once again, I saw this same kind of behavior. One former military officer that I was working with related to me that he was a Christian. I was in his quarters with him when he got on SKPYE and talked to his wife with two small children in the background. He had at least two girlfriends on the side that I knew of. I asked him if he thought this was good to be doing to his wife. I heard something like, "No, but I'm going to do it anyway. What Mama don't know won't hurt her."

These cases aren't the only times I've seen behavior like this. I've seen similar cases during my active military duty years as well. Secular behavior in the world may convey that you rate what you get away with, but it doesn't make it right. Sin always has its rewards, and the piper sooner or later comes to collect for the music in one way or another.

On a different note, just because someone says that they're a Christian, it doesn't necessarily mean that they have a personal relationship with Jesus Christ. Let us pretend to take a walk to a barn. You tell me that there's a donkey in the barn. As we get closer, I hear a "moo." You fooled me—you said that there was a donkey in the barn, but it's really a cow instead. So how do we really know if we love God? John 14:15 makes it pretty clear, "**If ye love me, keep my commandments**." Those who love God will try to honor and keep His Word. People will be known by their fruits.

God sees all. God knows all. One does not fool God. He knows the very hairs on our heads. One may think he can fool his wife or someone else, but one will not fool God. We should be zealous for good works, and serve God with our whole hearts. As Christians, we should talk the talk, and then walk the walk. We should, to the best of our ability, walk properly before God no matter where we are, or who we're with. The secular world may think we're peculiar for not doing things the secular way, but it's always best to put God and His Word first. God always takes priority.

Chapter 12
Preparation and Study Common

Preparation and study were common throughout my military career, whether preparing for an operation, or advancement in career. Each person, in reality, is to study the Word of God to know his/her role in the family, whether as husband or wife, parent or child. 2 Timothy 2:15 makes that pretty clear, "**Study to shew thyself approved unto God**, a workman that needeth not to be ashamed, rightly dividing the word of truth."

I learned that in military leadership, a commanding officer will guide, govern, and guard his personnel. He must provide leadership, establish goals, and make quality decisions, based on higher directives. He must govern to maintain proper functioning and fitness of his unit, and he must guard his personnel by ensuring they have the proper equipment and the right information to accomplish the mission.

As a godly husband, the man is to be head of his wife. Ephesians 5:23 states, "For the husband is the head of the wife, even as Christ is the head of the church: and he is the savior of the body." For a man, this means leadership. Godly leadership is needed in the family so the husband should live up to God-given responsibility. He should seek to guide, govern, and guard his home with the right attitude towards God and family.

A husband's headship must be exercised in love, humility, and consideration of his wife and her needs before himself. He is not to be a tyrant or dictator. His wife is not to be his slave and "bow" before him. They serve each other.

Let's share an example of initiating love and reconciliation. Perhaps the husband has had a spat with his wife in the course of the day. Both are upset with each other. However, the husband knows that he needs to get things right before going to bed. Thus, he approaches his wife to try to civilly talk things out. He asks for forgiveness and acknowledges any wrong. He seeks reconciliation because it's the godly thing to do.

On another note, the husband may notice that he and his wife have gotten away from the devotions that they would read together before going to bed. He then takes the initiative to make sure that he and his wife get back to their devotions. He knows reading their devotions sets the mode of unity between them and brings peace from the Word of God into their hearts before they retire for the evening.

A good military leader makes sure the needs of his troops are met. A godly man will try to provide for the needs of his family. A good military leader guides his troops, and a godly father will teach, love, and chasten his children with the right attitude of correction in accordance with the Word.

> *A good military leader makes sure the needs of his troops are met. A godly man will try to provide for the needs of his family.*

Now, back to the beginning of this chapter. In the military, there's a common phrase—Prior Preparation Prevents Poor Performance. That's true in the military, but also in the affairs of life, and for a Christian's walk. Study to show thyself approved. Ultimately, the husband will want to ensure that his home is Christ-centered and he does what he's able to do in order to make this the case.

Chapter 13
Stand Up for God

I was assigned in Afghanistan during 2011 in support of a Department of Defense operation. I was a civilian assigned to an active duty U.S. Army infantry unit. We were assigned to a camp southeast of Kabul.

I had good rapport with the U.S. Army officer in-charge of the unit. Often his unit would depart camp in mine-resistant ambush protected (MRAP) vehicles. MRAP vehicles were built to better withstand improvised explosive device (IED) attacks and ambushes. Even so, before his unit would go off camp in an MRAP vehicle, I asked if I could pray with the men for their protection. Sometimes I would also go off camp in the MRAPs.

I remember, early on, how some of the members would look at me with a slight smile or grin, as if to say *what's this guy doing?* In other words, not all received my overtures very well, perhaps thinking this really wasn't cool or politically correct.

However, as time progressed in theater, some of these men started to look for me before they left camp for me to pray for the unit. Some would say, "Where's Mr. Imhof?" "Isn't he going to pray for us?" Not one time did this unit hit an IED, or encounter an ambush when I was assigned to them. I can't say that for all the units assigned to the camp. We had more than one funeral service on camp for personnel who had lost their lives.

God is faithful. God honors prayer, and God protects. If I had been fearful of men's faces, I might not have prayed for them early on. I put that aside because I know that God is real, and He's in control. I believed in divine protection, and I believed in it for them.

As God put it on my heart to pray for this unit, I knew that I must be faithful, and put the looks aside. By doing this I was also letting them know that I was confident in the Lord and who I was in Him. In essence, I wouldn't let myself be shamed for being a Christian, but I would stand up for God, and their protection. I don't point to me, but give God all the praise. Ultimately, a man consistent in his conviction will be much more respected than an ungrounded individual who regularly changes to fit the situation and who goes along with the crowd.

Romans 1:16 says, **"For I am not ashamed of the gospel of Christ**: for it is the power of God unto salvation to every one that believeth; to the Jew first, and also to the Greek." Never be ashamed of the gospel for it is a priceless gift, and is to be truly cherished.

Many have grown up with the wrong image of God. Many see God as a mean God with a big bat just waiting to hit you if you step out of line or do something wrong. Sometimes people attribute the deeds of Satan to God, and that's so wrong. Let's make this simple—there's nothing good in the devil, and nothing bad in God. One will keep their theology right if one remembers that. Let's not confuse the two.

I remember the story of the prodigal son from Luke 15:11–32. Basically, the prodigal son asks his father to give him his portion of the family estate as an early inheritance. Once received, the son promptly sets off on a long journey to a distant land and begins to waste his wealth on riotous living. As his money runs out, a severe famine hits the country and the son finds himself in a dire situation. In humility, he eventually returns home to his father hoping that his father would make him as a hired servant. Little did he know that his father, in reality, was yearning for him to come home. The father joyfully embraces his son, kills the fatted calf, and hosts a celebration in honor of his return. His son, who was lost, has now come home. The father is jubilant.

You see, the father wasn't there to hit him with a bat when the prodigal son came home. No, the father sought reconciliation because of the **deep love that he had for his son**. This is such a **vivid example of our Heavenly Father's love for us**.

Many have suffered at the hands of an abusive parent. "You've made your bed, now live in it." No, there wasn't a reply from the father like this to his son who had humbled himself and come home. There was forgiveness and reconciliation. Many who grow up in homes with excessively critical parents often view God as holding a big bat, waiting to hit them when they get out of line. Many have never heard their father say to them, "I love you, Son, or I love you, Daughter." Thus, for some, it's hard to accept the love of their Heavenly Father, because of the lack of love and/or abuse that they experienced in their childhood.

Many may also recall the story of the lady caught in adultery in John 8:3–11. Some men brought the lady to Jesus asking what was to be done with her as the law would require her to be stoned. Jesus stooped down and wrote on the ground, and then rose up to address them after they kept questioning him. He said let him who has not sinned cast the first stone, and then He stooped back down and wrote on the ground again. One by one each man departed. The lady was left alone by her accusers as Jesus told her that He did not condemn her either, and to go and sin no more. In a short while, He knew that He would be going to the cross for her sins. Why? **It's because He did not seek condemnation but reconciliation**. That's the love of God for all mankind. God's a good God, and the devil is a bad devil. Don't confuse the two!

> *Let us all stand up for God, and serve Him to the best of our ability. He deserves our best because He gave His all for us.*

It's not hard to understand the love of God when one examines these two stories. It should be considered a privilege for all of us to stand up for God. Jesus stood up for us when He bore the stripes on His back and died on the cross for our sins. He took a brutal beating and suffered an excruciating death for us. Why? It was because of **His great love for us, and that He sought reconciliation for us with the Heavenly Father**.

Let us all stand up for God, and serve Him to the best of our ability. He deserves our best because He gave His all for us.

Various Underwater Demolition/ SEAL (BUD/S) Training Photos

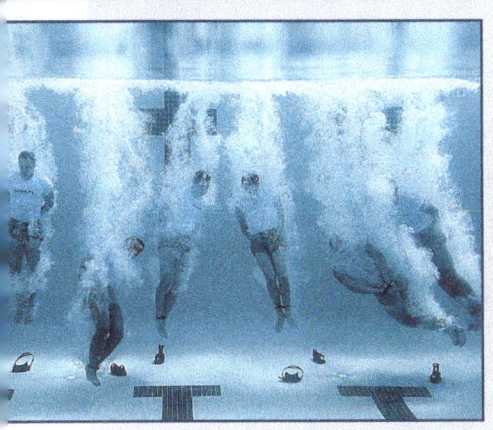

Various SEAL Photos

Various SEAL Photos (cont.)

Some Personal Photos

Some Ministry Photos

Some Ministry Photos (cont.)

One of My Favorite Paintings: *The Prayer at Valley Forge, by Arnold Friberg*

God's Hand was on America at its inception. Anyone who studies the life of George Washington can see this to be so. God consistently protected Washington so he could lead the colonies into becoming a great nation.

There are numerous accounts of the providence of God in George Washington's life. Given the task of taking Fort Duquesne during the French and Indian War (1754-1763) was British General Edward Braddock, a 65-year-old career soldier who had recently arrived in America from England. The year was 1755, and Braddock's senior American aide was a young colonel by the name of George Washington from the Virginia militia.

Braddock had trained his troops to fight European style—ignoring Washington's warnings—so they lined up in the open, shoulder to shoulder. The Indians and French, on the other hand, took cover behind rocks and trees, and began pouring a deadly fire down upon Braddock and his men during the Battle of Monongahela.

Most of the British and militia officers were killed, leaving Washington alone to command a broken and fleeing British army. In his book, *George Washington*, author William Roscoe Thayer relates how Washington rode to all parts of the field, trying to stem the retreat, and had two horses shot out from under him and four bullet holes in his coat. Mary Draper Ingles, in her biography, relates how the Indian Chief Red Hawk claimed to have shot at Washington eleven times, but did not succeed in killing him, despite his prowess for marksmanship. The Indians came to the conclusion that the "Great Spirit" was upon Washington.

Who can forget the Battle of Long Island on August 27, 1776? Washington had been soundly defeated by British General William Howe. Washington was chased near to the East River, across from Manhattan, and cornered. Howe placed a siege around Washington's forces, but did not immediately pursue after them.

Washington gathered as many boats as he could, under the cover of darkness, to ferry his outnumbered and tattered army across the river. He kept fires burning in camp to deceive the British. During the course of the night a mysterious fog somehow rolled in and helped conceal Washington's movements. The fog lifted after Washington and his men got across.

Then there was the Battle of Princeton on January 3, 1777. During one segment of the battle the inexperienced Colonists began to fall back under the steady fire of British regulars. As they were falling back, up rode Washington astride his horse. As he encouraged and rallied his troops amidst the flying musket balls, he came within 30 yards—easy musket range—of the British line.

For more information on Arnold Friberg's artwork,
visit www.fribergfineart.com

Chapter 13 One of My Favorite Paintings: 61

Washington remained uninjured despite his proximity to the British forces, and his galvanizing presence stabilized the Colonial line at a critical juncture in the battle. Washington, along with some reinforcements, were soon chasing remnants of the British forces through the fields and woods.

God's Hand of Divine Providence was clearly seen in these events and many more. Washington would acknowledge the providence of God in these situations, and on other occasions that would follow in the Revolutionary War. He knew the importance of God in the sustainment of his army and the forthcoming nation to be.

Conclusion

This book shared some important biblical principles that I learned from my military career. These principles help one live a better life, but they really won't amount to much unless one knows Jesus Christ as Lord and Savior. If there is any doubt as to your eternal destiny or salvation, then today, I urge you to consider the following scriptures.

"As it is written, There is none righteous, no, not one"
(Romans 3:10).

"For all have sinned, and come short of the glory of God"
(Romans 3:23).

"For the wages of sin is death; but the gift of God is eternal life through Jesus Christ our Lord"
(Romans 6:23).

"For there is one God, and one mediator between God and men, the man Christ Jesus"
(1 Timothy 2:5).

Chapter 13 Conclusion

"That if thou shalt confess with thy mouth the Lord Jesus, and shalt believe in thine heart that God hath raised him from the dead, thou shalt be saved. For with the heart man believeth unto righteousness; and with the mouth confession is made unto salvation"
(Romans 10:9–10).

Now, here's a Sinner's Prayer to receive Jesus as Lord and Savior. Please repeat the following prayer and mean it from your heart. You must be sincere or they will only be words, and mean nothing. If you are sincere, then God is sincere because God always honors His Word.

"Dear Heavenly Father, I come to You in the name of the Lord Jesus Christ. I ask You to forgive me of all my sins. I accept Jesus as my Lord and Savior and believe in my heart that He died on the cross for my sins, and that You raised Him from the dead so that I could have right standing with You. I now repent and confess Jesus as my Lord and Savior. I thank You for giving me eternal salvation and ask that You would help me in my Christian walk."

I strongly encourage you to read your Bible daily to get to know the Lord better, talk to God daily in prayer, and find a church where the Bible is taught as the complete Word of God. I also encourage you to be water baptized.

About the Author

Commander Michael H. Imhof, U.S. Navy (ret.), and former Navy SEAL, was born in Fort Bragg, North Carolina and raised in Blasdell, New York. He attended the State University College of New York at Buffalo, where he received a Bachelor of Science Degree. He was commissioned in 1973. After completing Basic Underwater Demolition/SEAL training in Coronado, California, Commander Imhof was assigned to SEAL Team TWO, subsequent Naval Special Warfare commands, and other duty assignments.

Commander Imhof, possessing a Naval Special Warfare designator, has served throughout the world in numerous positions. Assignments include Platoon Commander, Training Officer, Operations Officer, Staff Officer, Executive Officer and Commanding Officer. A graduate of the U.S. Army Special Forces Officer Qualification Course, he also earned a Master's Degree in Administration from George Washington University and served as an instructor at the U.S. Naval Academy. He has numerous service awards.

He has lived in Egypt, Jordan, Israel, Panama, South Korea, Liberia, Sudan, Somalia, Sinai and Afghanistan besides serving in numerous other countries throughout the world. On December 17, 1981, he was hijacked in Southern Lebanon while on duty with the United Nations Truce Supervision Organization. He believes his later escape was truly a blessing of God. A military officer of strong Christian convictions, Commander Imhof is ready and willing to share his faith with all. He is convinced that the Bible is the authoritative and uncompromised Word of God and gives thanks for the wonderful blessings of God in his life. He is the author of five Christian books.

We invite you to view the complete
selection of titles we publish at:
www.ASPECTBooks.com

We encourage you to write us
with your thoughts about this,
or any other book we publish at:
info@ASPECTBooks.com

ASPECT Books' titles may be purchased in
bulk quantities for educational, fund-raising,
business, or promotional use.
bulksales@ASPECTBooks.com

Finally, if you are interested in seeing
your own book in print, please contact us at:
publishing@ASPECTBooks.com

We are happy to review your manuscript at no charge.

www.ingramcontent.com/pod-product-compliance
Lightning Source LLC
Chambersburg PA
CBHW070559160426
43199CB00014B/2551